GUT- FRIENDLY FOODS

BY

KATHLEEN A. WILLIAMS

DISCLAIMER

The Publisher has strived to be as accurate and complete as possible in the creation of this report, notwithstanding the fact that she does not warrant or represent at any time that the contents within are accurate due to the rapidly changing nature of the Internet.

While all attempts have been made to verify information provided in this publication, the Publisher assumes no responsibility for errors, omissions, or contrary interpretation of the subject matter herein. Any perceived slights of specific persons, peoples, or organizations are unintentional.

In practical advice books, like anything else in life, there are no guarantees of income made. Readers are cautioned to reply on their own judgment about their individual circumstances to act accordingly.

This book is not intended for use as a source of legal, business, accounting or financial advice. All readers are advised to seek services of competent professionals in legal, business, accounting and finance fields.

You are encouraged to print this book for easy reading.

TABLE OF CONTENTS

CHAPTER 1

HOW TO IMPROVE GUT HEALTH

Your gut health can naturally be improved by eating the right foods and adopting healthy habits.

1. Consume Foods That Are High in Fiber and Probiotics

According to a study, fiber is a nutrient derived from plants that lower the risk of metabolic illnesses by promoting the diversity and proliferation of healthy bacteria in the gut. The fiber in sweet potatoes, spinach, beets, carrots, and fennel is naturally gut-beneficial. Whole grains are another excellent source of fiber in addition to fruits and vegetables.

Due to the probiotics they contain, fermented foods like yogurt, kimchi, sauerkraut, and kombucha are appreciated for their gut-healing properties. Particularly yogurt might improve gastrointestinal issues like constipation, inflammatory bowel illness, and diarrhea. According to one study, persons who consume yogurt frequently have more lactobacilli, a type of beneficial bacteria for the gut, as well as enterobacterium, a type of bacteria linked with inflammation.

2. Think About A Supplement

Probiotic pills are becoming more and more well-liked as awareness of the significance of gut health grows. Probiotic supplements aren't a cure-all for gut health, but there is some evidence that, in certain circumstances, they help improve the microbiota and restore gut health.

If your doctor has prescribed an antibiotic, they could also advise a probiotic supplement. There is proof that this might aid in preventing diarrhea brought on by antibiotics. Speak to your doctor about taking a probiotic supplement if you're interested. Despite a history of usage that appears to be safe, particularly in healthy individuals, the risk of negative consequences is higher in those with weakened immune systems.

3. Frequently Workout

Movement is therapeutic for a wide range of physiological systems, including the microbiota. Researchers have discovered that exercise encourages an increase in the diversity of good bacteria in the gut in both animal and human studies.

A 2019 review expressly stated that exercise can change the composition and functionality of gut bacteria independently of food, although much research highlight the complementary roles exercise and diet may play in positively altering gut health. Longer workouts and high-intensity aerobic exercise were found to have the greatest effects on gut bacteria diversity and function in connection to overall health. Additionally, they found that those who are lean are more likely than those who are overweight or obese to benefit from exercise's positive effects on gut health.

4. Reduce Your Alcohol Consumption

Your microbiota may also be badly impacted by excessive drinking. Recurrent alcohol consumption is connected to gastritis, an inflammation of the gut that irritates. Heartburn, ongoing discomfort, ulcers, and bacterial infections can all result from such inflammation.

Additionally, excessive drinking is linked to intestinal inflammation, which is an indication of a bad gut. According to research, this form of inflammation can upset the microbiota's balance and change how well it functions.

5. Lessen Your Stress Levels

Think about the butterflies you get when you're excited or anxious to understand that stress isn't only mental. The "gut-brain connection" and the gut's status as "the second brain" are frequently mentioned by experts in gut health. Although we don't fully understand their relationship, we do know that mental health and the gut are closely related.

IBS can increase the risk of anxiety and depression, and those who have IBS are more likely to experience these mental health issues, according to research.

Finding techniques to control your stress and mental health may help you get rid of unpleasant GI symptoms and restore balance to your body. Not sure where to begin? Consider including some exercise in your day. A daily walk could help your gut health since evidence indicates that exercise can enhance the quantity and quality of gut microorganisms that are good for your health.

CHAPTER 2

WHAT DOES "GUT MICROBIOME" MEAN?

The microorganisms that reside in your intestines are referred to as your "gut microbiome." Every person has a digestive system that contains roughly 200 different types of bacteria, viruses, and fungi. Many microbes are highly helpful and even necessary for a healthy body, while some are toxic to human health.

According to research, a diverse population of gut bacteria may lower the risk of diseases like diabetes, inflammatory bowel disease, and psoriatic arthritis.

What Impact Does Your Gut Microbiome Have On Your Health?

The medical world is conducting more research on the gut's amazing complexity and significance to our general health. Over the past few decades, studies have discovered connections between gut health and:

the defense mechanism, mentally sound, autoimmune condition, endocrine dysfunction, an intestinal condition, cardiovascular condition, and cancer.

There may be a link between greater gut bacterial diversity and better health. Even though research is still in progress, it is evident that many aspects of your health and wellbeing are influenced by the condition of your gut.

Indicators Of A Bad Gut.

Your gut microbiome can be impacted by many aspects of modern living, including: *high levels of stress, consuming a Western diet heavy in processed and high-sugar foods, getting insufficient sleep, and using antibiotics.*

Your health in turn may be impacted in different ways, including: *immunological response, hormone amounts, and weight-related illness development.*

If your gut health is compromised, you might experience a few symptoms. Below are some of the most typical symptoms:

1. A Queasy Stomach

Disturbances in digestion can all be indicators of gut disease. They consist of: constipation, bloating, gas constipation, and heartburn. A balanced gut will likely experience fewer symptoms as it processes food and waste more easily.

2. A Diet High In Sugar

The quantity and variety of "good" bacteria in your stomach can be decreased by a diet high in processed foods and added sugars. According to research, this can cause the body's inflammation to grow. Numerous diseases, including cancer, can have inflammation as a precursor.

3. Unintentional Changes In Weight

Weight fluctuations without a change in food or exercise routine could indicate a problem with your digestive system. Your body's capacity to absorb nutrients, control blood sugar, and store fat can all be hampered by an unbalanced gut.

Mal-absorption brought on a small intestine bacterial overgrowth (SIBO) may result in weight loss. Alternatively, weight gain could result from either insulin resistance or elevated inflammation.

4. Sleep Issues Or Persistent Exhaustion

According to research, a gut-bacterial imbalance may be associated with short sleep durations and fragmented sleep patterns, which may result in chronic exhaustion. While the reason is still unknown. Persistent exhaustion seems to be related to metabolic activity, inflammation, and mental wellness.

5. Skin Sensitivity

There may be a connection between certain types of gut bacteria and skin diseases like psoriasis. The immune system of the body may be impacted by lower levels of helpful bacteria. Conditions that affect the organs, including the skin, may result from this in turn.

6. Auto-immune Disorders

The immune system and the gut have been linked in numerous research. an unwell gut may make the immune system less effective and cause systemic inflammation. Auto-immune illnesses can result from this, in which the body defends itself rather than dangerous invaders.

7. Food Sensitivities

Food intolerances are brought on by problems with particular meals' digestion. Contrary to food allergies, which are brought on by an immune system response to certain foods, this is different. According to research, dietary intolerances like lactose intolerance may be brought on by bad gut flora. This may cause issues with digestion of the trigger meals as well as symptoms like: gas, diarrhea, pain in the abdomen, and nausea. Additionally, several studies suggest that gut health and food allergies may be connected.

CHAPTER 3

FOODS FERMENTED FOR GUTTERA HEALTH

Foods or beverages created through managed microbial growth and enzymatic conversion of food components are referred to as fermented foods. In the past, a wide variety of foods, including meat and fish, dairy, vegetables, soybeans, other legumes, cereals, and fruits, underwent fermentation.

There are countless types of fermented meals thanks to the microorganisms, nutritional components, and environmental factors that all play a role in the fermentation process. Because the production of antimicrobial metabolites (such as organic acids, ethanol, and bacteriocins) lowers the danger of contamination with pathogenic bacteria, food fermentation has historically been used as a preservation technique. Additionally, fermentation is employed to improve the organoleptic qualities (e.g., taste and texture), Some foods, like olives, cannot be consumed without fermentation because it gets rid of the bitter phenolic components.

Foods are fermented using one of two main techniques. First, foods can naturally ferment; this process is frequently referred to as "wild fermentation" or "spontaneous fermentation," and it occurs when microorganisms are present in the raw food or processing environment naturally. Examples of such foods include sauerkraut, kimchi, and some fermented soy products. Second, meals can be fermented by adding "culture-dependent ferments," such as kefir, kombucha, and natto, which are starter cultures that are used to start the fermentation process.

Backslopping is a technique for carrying out a culture-dependent ferment in which a little quantity of a previously fermented batch is introduced to the uncooked food, such as sourdough bread. Fermentation starters can be either natural or artificial (for instance, backslopping), or chosen commercial starters to uniformize the organoleptic properties of the finished product.

Almost every cuisine in the world includes fermented foods in some form. Fermented foods have seen a rise in popularity in the West in recent years, largely due to claims that they provide health benefits and the growing interest in gastrointestinal health. Fermented foods may have positive impacts on health and disease via several processes.

They first contain micro-organisms that may be probiotic, like lactic acid bacteria. The majority of fermented foods have been reported to have at least 106 microbial cells per gram, while concentrations can vary depending on the product's area, processing method, and other factors, age, and the period during which the products are examined or consumed. Through its buffering and protective action against intestinal circumstances (such as low pH, and bile acids), the surrounding food matrix appears to have a significant influence on the survival of probiotic strains.

In fact, several investigations have demonstrated that bacteria from fermented foods can enter the gastrointestinal tract; however, this is likely to vary amongst products, and their presence in the gut appears to be temporary. However, by competing with pathogenic bacteria and producing immune-regulatory and neurogenic fermentation byproducts, these microorganisms may still be able to exert a physiological advantage in the gut.

Metabolites produced during fermentation may have positive effects on health. For instance, lactic acid bacteria produce bioactive peptides and polyamines that may have an impact on metabolic, immunological, and cardiovascular health and are applicable to both dairy and non-dairy fermented foods.

Certain substances may undergo fermentation and become physiologically active metabolites. For instance, phenolic substances (like flavonoids) can be transformed by lactic acid bacteria into physiologically active metabolites.

Nutrients included in fermented foods, like prebiotics and vitamins, may also have positive effects on health. Fermentation can lower levels of toxins and anti-nutrients. For instance, fermenting soybeans may lower levels of phytic acid, and fermenting sourdough may lower levels of fermentable carbohydrates (such as fermentable oligosaccharides, disaccharides, monosaccharides, and polyols, or FODMAPs), which may increase the risk of developing food allergies patients with functional bowel disorders like irritable bowel syndrome on their ability to tolerate these products.

Eating foods that have undergone fermentation has numerous health advantages. Fermented foods have wonderful health advantages for your body, and they may hold the secret to higher immunity, better digestion, and more energy. A healthy body depends greatly on a healthy stomach.

Foods For Good Gut Health

1. Yogurt

Probiotics, commonly referred to as "friendly bacteria," are abundant in live yogurt. For a good breakfast, look for variants with full fat and no added sugar. Yogurt drinks may contain far higher concentrations of probiotic bacteria than a typical yogurt, which is helpful for the digestive system. However, keep in mind that they may contain a lot of sugar.

2. Kefir

This probiotic beverage is created by fermenting milk and is brimming with beneficial bacteria (which can help to reduce a leaky gut). The hilly area between Asia and Europe, as well as Central Asia and Russia, is where it first appeared. You can also use it as the foundation for salad dressing or as a fantastic addition to smoothies and soups (add lemon juice and seasoning).

3. Miso

Miso is produced using matured soya beans, in addition to grain or rice, and contains a scope of treats like supportive microbes and proteins. An exquisite glue utilized in plunges, dressings, and soup, it can likewise be utilized as a marinade for salmon or tofu. It's a staple of Japanese cooking and reasonable in the event that you're keeping away from dairy. There is vulnerability inside the examination that the microscopic organisms arrive at the stomach, in any case in locales where Miso is a staple matured food source, the populace has better stomach wellbeing and less gut sickness.

4. Sauerkraut

This is finely cleaved cabbage that has been aged. This extraordinary wellspring of probiotics, fiber, and nutrients are most popular as a German dish, yet forms exist in Eastern and Central Europe. Pick an item that has not been salted in vinegar, as that doesn't have similar advantages. It's flavorful presented with hotdogs and can be modest and simple to make at home.

5. Kimchi

This Korean specialty of aged vegetables brings the advantages of probiotic microscopic organisms alongside nutrients and fiber. Use it as an enthusiastic side dish with meat, salad, or eggs. It's famous to the point that Koreans say "kimchi" similarly to that we say "cheddar" when they have their photographs taken.

6. Sourdough

This is truly popular right now, yet there's a valid justification for that. Made by maturing the batter, it's more edible than normal bread and its energy delivers gradually. It makes fabulous toast as well.

7. Almonds

These have great probiotic properties, and that implies they are a treat for your stomach microorganisms - high in fiber and brimming with unsaturated fats and polyphenols. A modest bunch of almonds makes a great bite while you're feeling peckish.

8. Olive Oil

Stomach microscopic organisms and stomach microorganisms like an eating routine of unsaturated fats and polyphenols. These are tracked down in olive oil. Studies have shown that it diminishes stomach aggravation. Use it for salad dressing or shower it over cooked vegetables. A few examinations have likewise observed olive oil to be gainful in facilitating heartburn issues and can likewise help your pancreas by bringing its necessity down to deliver stomach-related catalysts.

9. Fermented Tea

We as a whole realize water is critical for stomach wellbeing, however what else could you at any point drink? The fermented tea is a matured tea drink remembered to have begun in Manchuria that is brimming with probiotic great microscopic organisms. It has a sharp, vinegary taste and can be utilized as an invigorating beverage all alone or blended in with leafy foods. It likewise makes the base for extraordinary mixed drinks.

10. Peas

Stomach microscopic organisms need fiber to thrive, so the more foods grown from the ground you devour the better. Peas are brimming with solvent and insoluble fiber to assist with keeping your framework in balance. Add peas to sautés, soups, or mixed greens.

11. Brussels sprouts

Substantially more than a bubbly staple, they contain the sorts of fiber that great microorganisms like sulfur intensify which assist with combatting undesirable microbes like H pylori. Pan sear with garlic and bacon for a flavorful side dish.

12. Bananas

One of nature's handiest and best bites, bananas are loaded with the sort of fiber that great microscopic organisms appreciate. They likewise contain solid minerals.

13. Roquefort Cheddar

Live, runny, foul French cheese will give your stomach microscopic organisms a lift - however, eat it with some restraint. Add it to plates of mixed greens or spread it on your sourdough. While we can't be guaranteed that all of the helpful micro-organisms can survive digesting, it's thought that the additional qualities aid in the preservation of some bacteria during digestion.

14. Garlic

With its anti-bacterial and anti-fungal qualities, garlic can help regulate "bad" gut flora and balance intestinal yeast. Add it to savory foods as a flavoring. The compounds in garlic serve as a fuel source for the bacteria, enhancing their performance and enhancing gut health in the process.

15. Ginger

Fresh ginger stimulates the digestive tract to keep food moving through the intestines and can aid in the generation of stomach acid. Add freshly grated ginger to smoothies, stir-fries, soups, and stews. To create hydrating ginger tea, pour boiling water over grated ginger.

CHAPTER 4

PREBIOTICS

Prebiotic food sources contain more mind-boggling carbs (like inulin, an insoluble kind of fiber) which are aged in our stomach and produce metabolites called short-chain unsaturated fats that feed and support the "great micro-organisms" in our gastrointestinal system.

These short-chain unsaturated fats are consumed by the cells in our gastrointestinal coating and are the primary wellspring of supplements for those cells. Short-chain unsaturated fats, for example, butyric corrosive, assist with keeping our stomach's major areas of strength from obstruction and decreasing irritation.

Prebiotic Rich Foods Include:

Asparagus, Chickpeas, Onions, Almonds and Nuts Fresh Fruits (Raspberries, apples, blueberries, blackberries, and so on) Quinoa and Other Whole Grains, Sweet Potatoes, Artichokes Broccoli and Cruciferous, Vegetables, and Bananas.

Other Surprising Gut Health Foods

By the end of the day, you'll constantly see the most advantages from eating a fair eating routine wealthy in entire products of the soil, however, the following are a couple of different food sources you can add to assist with supporting your stomach-related wellbeing.

1. Endlessly Ginger Beer

Customarily, blended ginger or root brew is arranged in the same way as fermented tea; a harmonious settlement of yeast and lactobacillus microorganisms helps with maturing the ginger, sugar, and water into a delectable carbonated drink.

Ginger has been utilized for ages as a characteristic home solution for calming stomach related disturbances, and because of current logical investigations, we now realize that ginger makes different remedial impacts. Ginger contains cancer prevention agents, calming, and immuno-strong mixtures.

This probiotic-filled soft drink might be a superior decision over other elective sweet carbonated refreshments. Sugnificantly, ginger brews can contain an undesirable overabundance of sugars; plan to track down a brand with as little sugar as could be expected, or like any food that is a piece sweet, go for the gold! Ginger brew and soda are utilized conversely to allude to a matured ginger pop; ginger lager will in general be more grounded in flavor.

2. Grown Grains

Grown grains allude to grain or seed that has been previously absorbed in water, and afterward saved soggy for a particular measure of time until it starts to grow.

They are considered as superfood because the course of germination expands the focus and bio-availability of nutrients and minerals like folate, fiber, L-ascorbic acid, zinc, magnesium, and B nutrients. You can grow your fledglings at home or get some from the supermarket. They are perfect to blend into servings of mixed greens, mix fries, and make heavenly in-a-hurry snacks.

Assuming that you buy items that contain fledglings, for example, grown bread or tortillas, know that they may not contain a similar measure of supplements as the crude fledgling itself because of the assembling system. "Superfood" or "utilitarian food" are unregulated terms prevalently used to allude to food sources that might give benefits past their dietary benefit, such as further developing stomach wellbeing or bringing down circulatory strain.

3. Bone Broth

For quite a while, it's been conjectured that custom-made bone stock can uphold your wellbeing. You've most likely known about the "chicken soup" solution for colds and influenza as bone stocks are not difficult to process and are accepted to have recuperating capacities.

This hypothesis is somewhat back-by science as the facts confirm that natively constructed bone stock contains bio-available collagen, and effortlessly processed amino acids, nutrients, minerals, and fundamental unsaturated fats, however just in limited quantities. The sort and measure of amino acids and supplements can likewise fluctuate in light of the kind of bones utilized, how long the stock is cooked, and how much handling (assuming it's canned or bundled).

Truly bone stock isn't a panacea, there isn't sufficient logical exploration yet to guarantee bone stock alone will recuperate your stomach, help your resistance, or fix the disease. Although, most examinations have zeroed in on noticing the advantages of ingesting detached types of collagen or gelatin for skin and joint wellbeing, not bone stocks explicitly for stomach wellbeing.

Bone stocks can be a superb choice to calm an irritated stomach and decrease the weight of processing on your body.

4. Avocados

Avocados are high in Omega-3 unsaturated fats, explicitly alpha-linolenic unsaturated fats. Integrating these sound mon-ounsaturated fats into your eating routine can assist you with feeling more satisfied, diminish irritation, and emphatically impact your cholesterol levels.

Eating more omega-3-rich food sources might advance microbiome variety, while additionally expanding the development of calming mixtures and supporting the wellbeing of our gastrointestinal cell wall.

They additionally contain valuable measures of fiber, potassium, L-ascorbic acid, and vitamin E. Basically, 1 medium avocado gives more than 10 grams of fiber. Regardless of whether you're group avocado, expanding your admission of entire food varieties gives your stomach helpful supplements and fiber.

5. Chicory Root

Chicory root is a stringy rhizome reaped from a plant in the daisy family. It is usually heated, ground, and utilized as an espresso substitute or fiber-added substance because of its high grouping of inulin, one of the prebiotic intensities in chicory.

Alongside useful prebiotic compounds, chicory root has different minerals like potassium, calcium, magnesium, selenium, and zinc. The roots have a harsh taste however, drinking chicory root espresso or involving it as a useful food fix while baking, or making protein shakes, helps most conform to the flavor.

CHAPTER 5

MITIGATING FOODS

Inflammation can be both great and awful. On one hand, it assists your body in protecting itself from disease and injury. Then again, persistent irritation can prompt infection. Stress, low movement levels, and food sources that cause inflammation make this hazard considerably more prominent.

Notwithstanding, studies propose that a few food varieties can assist in diminishing constant inflammation. The following are 13 mitigating food varieties:

1. Berries

Berries are little organic products that are loaded with fiber, nutrients, and minerals. Many assortments exist. The absolute most normal ones include: strawberries, blueberries, raspberries, and blackberries. Berries contain cell reinforcements called anthocyanins. These mixtures have calming impacts that might decrease your chance of sickness.

In one review including 25 grown-ups, the people who consumed blueberry powder consistently delivered essentially more regular executioner cells (NK cells) than the individuals who didn't consume the powder. These discoveries were like those of a more established study. Your body normally delivers NK cells, and they assist with keeping your safety framework working appropriately.

In another review, grown-ups with excess weight who ate strawberries had lower levels of specific fiery markers related to coronary illness than the people who didn't eat strawberries.

2. Fatty fish

Greasy fish are an incredible wellspring of protein and the long-chain omega-3 unsaturated fats eicosapentaenoic acid (EPA) and docosahexaenoic acid (DHA). Although a wide range of fish contain some omega-3 unsaturated fats, these greasy fish are among the best sources: Salmon, sardines, herring, mackerel, anchovies.

EPA and DHA assist with decreasing aggravation, which may somehow or another lead to metabolic disorder, coronary illness, diabetes, and kidney infection. Your body processes these unsaturated fats into compounds called resolvins and proteins, which have calming impacts.

Investigations have discovered that individuals consuming salmon or EPA and DHA supplements experienced decreases in the fiery marker C-reactive protein (CRP). In one review, individuals with a sporadic heartbeat who took EPA and DHA every day encountered no distinction in fiery markers compared to those who got a fake treatment.

3. Broccoli

Broccoli is very nutritious. It's a cruciferous vegetable, alongside cauliflower, brussels fledglings, and kale. Research has shown that eating a ton of cruciferous vegetables is related to a diminished risk of coronary illness and disease . This might be connected to the mitigating impacts of the cell reinforcements they contain.

Broccoli is rich in sulforaphane, a cancer prevention agent that diminishes aggravation by decreasing your levels of cytokines and atomic variable kappa B (NF-B), which are particles that drive irritation in your body.

4. Avocados

Avocados are loaded with potassium, magnesium, fiber, and heart-solid monounsaturated fats. They likewise contain carotenoids and tocopherols, which are connected to a diminished risk of disease. Moreover, one compound in avocados might diminish aggravation in recently formed skin cells.

In one excellent review incorporating 51 grown-ups with excess weight, the people who ate avocado for a long time had a decrease in provocative markers like interleukin 1 beta (IL-1) and CRP.

5. Green tea

You've most likely heard that green tea is quite possibly one of the best refreshments you can drink. Research has observed, that drinking it is related to a decreased risk of coronary illness, malignant growth, Alzheimer's infection, heftiness, and different circumstances. Quite a lot of its advantages are because of its cell reinforcement and calming properties, particularly a substance called epigallocatechin-3-gallate (EGCG).

EGCG represses aggravation by lessening supportive of provocative cytokine creation and harm to the unsaturated fats in your cells.

6. Peppers

Ringer peppers and stew peppers are stacked with L-ascorbic acid and cell reinforcements that make strong mitigating impacts. Chime peppers also contain the cell reinforcement quercetin, which may alleviate the symptoms of chronic illnesses such as diabetes. Stew peppers contain sinapic corrosive and ferulic corrosive, which might decrease irritation and promote better maturing.

7. Mushrooms

Many assortments of mushrooms exist around the world, only a couple are palatable and developed financially. These incorporate truffles, portobello mushrooms, and shiitake mushrooms. Mushrooms are extremely low in calories and rich in selenium, copper, and all of the B nutrients.

They additionally contain phenols and different cancer prevention agents that give mitigating insurance. An extraordinary sort of mushroom called lion's mane may possibly lessen second-rate irritation connected with stoutness.

Nonetheless, one investigation discovered that cooking mushrooms brought down their calming compounds fundamentally. Consequently, it could be ideal to eat them crudely or delicately cooked.

8. Grapes

Grapes contain anthocyanins, which decrease aggravation. Also, they might reduce the risk of a few sicknesses, including coronary illness, diabetes, corpulence, Alzheimer's, and eye problems. Grapes are also one of the best sources of resveratrol, another cell-renewal compound with numerous medical benefits.

Concentrates show that resveratrol can safeguard the heart against irritation. In one review incorporating 60 individuals with cardiovascular breakdown, the people who consumed two 50-mg containers of resveratrol day to day for quite some time encountered a lessening in provocative quality markers, including interleukin 6 (IL-6).

9. Turmeric

Turmeric is a zest with a warm, gritty flavor that is often utilized in curries and other Indian dishes. It has gotten a great deal of consideration since it contains curcumin, a strong calming compound. Research has shown that turmeric lessens irritation connected with joint inflammation, diabetes, and different illnesses.

In one review, individuals with metabolic disorder consumed 1 gram of curcumin day to day joined with piperine from dark pepper. They encountered a critical diminishing in the provocative marker CRP. It could be difficult to get enough curcumin from turmeric alone to encounter a recognizable impact. Taking enhancements containing disconnected curcumin might be considerably more viable.

Curcumin supplements are frequently joined with piperine, which can help curcumin retention by 2,000%. More examination is expected to comprehend what the measurement of turmeric means for incendiary markers.

10. Additional virgin olive oil

Additional virgin olive oil is quite possibly the best fat you can eat. It's wealthy in mon-ounsaturated fats and a staple in the Mediterranean eating regimen, which gives various medical advantages. Concentrates on interface additional virgin olive oil to a diminished gamble of coronary illness, cerebrum disease, and other serious medical issues.

In one concentrate on the Mediterranean eating regimen, CRP and a few other provocative markers fundamentally diminished in the people who consumed 1.7 ounces (50 mL) of olive oil consistently for quite a long time.

The impact of oleocanthal, a cancer prevention agent found in olive oil, has been contrasted with calming drugs like ibuprofen. Remember that additional virgin olive oil has more prominent calming benefits than refined olive oils.

11. Dull chocolate and cocoa

Dull chocolate is delectable, rich, and fulfilling. It's additionally loaded with cancer prevention agents that assist with lessening irritation. These may diminish your gamble of infection and lead to better maturing. Flavanols are answerable for chocolate's calming impacts and assist with keeping the endothelial cells that line your courses solid.

In one little review, individuals who consumed 350 mg of cocoa flavanols two times everyday experienced superior vascular capability following fourteen days.

12. Tomatoes

The tomato is a dietary force to be reckoned with. Tomatoes are high in L-ascorbic acid, potassium, and lycopene, a cancer prevention agent with amazing mitigating properties. Lycopene might be especially advantageous for decreasing support of fiery mixtures connected with a few sorts of disease.

Note that cooking tomatoes in olive oil can assist you with engrossing a greater amount of their lycopene content. That is on the grounds that lycopene is a carotenoid, a supplement that is better caught up with a wellspring of fat.

13. Cherries

Cherries are scrumptious and wealthy in cancer prevention agents, for example, anthocyanins and catechins, which decline irritation. Albeit the wellbeing, advancing properties of tart cherries have been concentrated on more than different assortments, sweet cherries additionally give benefits.

One review including 37 more established grown-ups found that the individuals who drank 16 ounces (480 mL) of tart cherry squeeze everyday for a very long time experienced fundamentally lower levels of the incendiary marker CRP. Another review found tart cherry juice affected irritation in sound more youthful grown-ups after they took it everyday for 30 days.

Incendiary Food Sources

As well as filling your eating routine with nutritious calming fixings, it's essential to restrict your utilization of food sources that can advance irritation. For instance, super handled food varieties like cheap food, frozen dinners, and handled meats have been related with higher blood levels of provocative markers like CRP.

In the interim, seared food sources and to some degree hydrogenated oils contain trans fats, a kind of unsaturated fat that examination has connected to expanded degrees of irritation. Different food varieties like sugar-improved drinks and refined carbs have additionally been displayed to advance aggravation.

Here are a few instances of food sources that have been connected to expanded degrees of irritation:

- Handled food varieties: potato chips and inexpensive food.
- Refined carbs: white breads, white rice, saltines, and rolls.
- Fried food varieties: fries, seared chicken, and mozzarella sticks.
- Sugar-improved refreshments: pop, sweet tea, and sports drinks.
- Processed meats: bacon, ham, and sausages.

- Trans fats: shortening and margarine.

Remember that it's fit as a fiddle to eat these incidentally. Simply attempt to guarantee that you follow an even eating routine that depends on entire food sources, including bunches of products of the soil. It's ideal to adhere to food sources that are insignificantly handled.

CHAPTER 6

BEST FOODS FOR WEIGHT LOSS

Assuming that you're attempting to get thinner, you might be enticed to cut calories, however eating too little can endanger your wellbeing. As a matter of fact, research shows an eating regimen of under 1,000 calories daily for the most part neglects to give the decent sustenance your body needs, and it can prompt nutrient and mineral insufficiencies related with serious wellbeing issues.

In addition, eating far less calories than you really want makes your body separate its own muscle and organ tissues for fuel. What's more, the less lean tissue mass you have, the slower your metabolic rate, which isn't great for weight reduction.

So rather than confining your caloric intake, center around taking care of your body better food varieties — it's a more powerful weight reduction system. Here are the best food sources to help a solid and practical weight reduction plan:

1. Lean Protein

Lean protein sources like chicken, turkey and grass-took care of lean meat assist with keeping you full, decline desires and settle glucose.. Plant-based proteins like vegetables, beans and lentils have similar advantages, and they're high in fiber too, so they advance satiety.

2. Eggs

Eggs contain pretty much every fundamental nutrient (except for Vitamin C), in addition to minerals like phosphorus, calcium and potassium. Alongside being a wellspring of complete protein, eggs are likewise versatile for various preferences.

3. Vegetables

Vegetables can help with weight reduction. For instance, cruciferous vegetables like broccoli, cauliflower, Brussels fledglings and cabbage are high in fiber and nutrients and assist with diminishing stomach related issues. In the interim, dim green verdant vegetables contain protein and are a decent wellspring of nutrients, minerals and fiber. Furthermore, crunchy vegetables like celery and jicama are incredible low-calorie choices for eating.

4. Avocados

Avocados are completely underestimated. The natural product is high in fiber and is a quality wellspring of sound fat, making it an extraordinary nourishment for diminishing yearning. In any case, since it is a fat source, avocado is calorically thick, so it's vital to stay aware of part size.

5. Apples

Apples are high in fiber and cancer prevention agents. The natural product likewise has mitigating properties and contains phytochemicals and L-ascorbic acid.

6. Berries

Berries are high in fiber, cancer prevention agents and L-ascorbic acid — everything that your body needs to work ideally.

7. Nuts and Seeds

Nuts and seeds have different medical advantages. All nuts are a decent wellspring of fiber, protein and solid fat, and they assist with diminishing craving. In the interim, seeds are an extraordinary wellspring of minerals and sound fat. Watch your parts here, as well. One serving of nuts and seeds is comparable to a quarter cup.

8. Salmon

Salmon is high in protein and omega-3 unsaturated fats. Research proposes omega-3 unsaturated fats might assist individuals with weight delegated overweight or stoutness feel fuller. What's more, fish overall might assist you with feeling fulfilled and more full longer than different proteins like eggs and meat.

9. Shrimp

Shrimp advances expanded sensations of satiety. Eating shrimp seems to diminish hunger by invigorating the creation of cholecystokinin, or CCK, a chemical that signs to your stomach that you're fulfilled. Additionally, shrimp and other shellfish contain zinc and selenium, two significant minerals for safe wellbeing and expanded energy.

10. Lupini Beans

Lupini beans are high in prebiotic fiber that takes care of the valuable microscopic organisms in your stomach. At the point when your stomach's microscopic organisms are very much sustained, the number and kind of microorganisms present increases. A very much populated and different microbiome further develops stomach wellbeing, which makes your cells more receptive to insulin, assisting with eliminating fat put away around the midsection.

11. Unripe Bananas

Unripe bananas contain one of the world's most extravagant wellsprings of prebiotic-safe starch. Prebiotic-safe starch makes your cells more receptive to insulin, assisting with forestalling fat capacity around your waistline. Joined with protein (in a smoothie with a protein powder as well as nut spread), it can keep you fulfilled for a really long time.

12. Whole Oats

Whole oats are brimming with safe starch — a kind of starch that opposes processing — which is a very weight reduction cordial. During the time spent on absorption, safe starch discharges results that can make your cells more receptive to insulin, assisting with decreasing difficult fat around your midriff.

13. Sauerkraut

Sauerkraut, or matured cabbage, is both a prebiotic and probiotic food, meaning it adds helpful microscopic organisms to your gastrointestinal parcel and feeds the great micro-organisms. Sauerkraut is likewise high in fiber, helping control hunger and manage blood glucose levels.

14. Vegetables

Vegetables decidedly affect satiety and stomach wellbeing. Their high fiber content keeps you feeling more full for longer, which forestalls gorging. In addition, they contain supplements that support your stomach's microscopic organisms, as well.

15. Chia Seeds

Chia seeds can assist with weight control in two ways. In the first place, they're stacked with fiber that can assist you with feeling full, forestalling gorging. Second, they extend in water, so on the off chance that you eat them in their unsoaked structure, they fill in your stomach, occupying more room and turning into a characteristic craving suppressant.

16. Water

Water isn't a food, yet it's similarly significant with regards to sound weight reduction. All of our body processes need water to work — digestion is one of these cycles, so be certain to remain very much hydrated.

CONCLUSION

Keeping a sound stomach is vital to better wellbeing and insusceptibility. Changes to your eating routine, like eating suitable measures of probiotics, prebiotics and strands and keeping away from sugars and antitoxins, can do wonders for your wellbeing and even work on your personal satisfaction.

Continuously remember, that what you eat as its for your actual wellbeing as well as for the numerous accommodating microscopic organisms that live in our stomach. Go with the ideal decision for a better stomach and a better you.

www.ingramcontent.com/pod-product-compliance
Lightning Source LLC
LaVergne TN
LVHW020536160826
845677LV00015B/4101

* 9 7 9 8 8 4 6 4 9 9 4 6 1 *